Coaching

9 Powerful Laws of Transformational Coaching

(coaching mindset, coaching books, coaching habit, coaching laws, team coaching)

by Jonathan C. Adler

Table of Contents

Enjoy your Free Books and VIP Access to Diamonds Book Club!

Introduction

Chapter 1 – Awareness

Chapter 2 – The Essential Self

Chapter 3 – Leaps of Faith

Chapter 4 – Embracing Being

Chapter 5 – The Hierarchy of Commitment

Chapter 6 – Methods and Tools

Conclusion

Disclaimer

While all attempts have been made to verify the information provided in this book, the author does not assume any responsibility for errors, omissions, or contrary interpretations of the subject matter contained within. The information provided in this book is for educational and entertainment purposes only. The reader is responsible for his or her own actions and the author does not accept any responsibilities for any liabilities or damages, real or perceived, resulting from the use of this information.

Thank you for purchasing my book!
FREE AND EXCLUSIVE TO SUBSCRIBERS

YOUR FREE GIFT!

Want to become a VIP Member of our Diamonds Book Club?

Your personal development is important for us and we want to offer you exclusive access to Diamonds Book Club. You will get instant access to our VIP list with free books, promotions and giveaways.

Enjoy your Free Books and VIP Access to Diamonds Book Club!

To your success!

https://forms.aweber.com/form/64/1045768564.htm

Introduction

As we become adults and move into our worlds of work, family, personal interests and so on, we find there is a tension between what we desire for ourselves and what life has given us.

Often, for many of us, the demands of nearly everything outside of us take precedent over our own personal needs and desires. Work drives our daily schedules.

The needs of our families take over our own personal growth. Social dictates determine how we are to behave in the day to day world. At some point, these things can overwhelm us and threaten to diminish our very sense of Self.

With the rise of professional life coaching we have learned that with the proper guidance, with a specific regimen of realistic and long-term goals, and with a re-directed outlook on life, it is possible to take our lives back and begin living on our own terms

A transformative life coach is an expert trained to guide people toward realizing their most essential life goals. They help clients reveal their own unique vision of themselves and their lives and provide one on one careful guidance for how understand, formulate, and attain that personal vision.

Life coaching is distinguished form therapy, for instance, in that therapy focuses almost exclusively on guidance for highly specific internal issues and problems; finding the source of those issues and ultimately helping a person learn how to overcome them.

Transformative life coaching, by contrast, is aimed at reaching far-reaching life goals. While a transformative live coaches will work with many of the same internal issues and a therapist, they are more attuned to utilizing the internal structure of being in guiding clients toward a mode of live which is goal oriented.

People who seek the help of a life coach are frequently at a crossroads in life. They have met resistance in one aspect of their lives or another and have come to see more adversity that possibility. The role of the transformative life coach is to reveal the possibilities inherent in those adversities.

There are some key elements to life coaching that seem to cross every model of life coaching at work today.

What we might call the nine powerful laws of transformational life coach consist of Identity, defining the inside and the outside, limiting negative beliefs, empowering beliefs, understanding fear, transforming fear, realization, identify, and empowerment.

Each of these tends to blend in with the others and these laws do not remain distinct categories largely because transformational life coaching is by definition an holistic approach to life management. As we will see, our understanding of identity has everything to do with how we define our inner worlds in relation to our outer world.

What is more, the path to understanding fear is actually one of the key methods for transforming fear. Ultimately, as we move through each of these laws as life coaches, we inevitably end up with the empowerment at the end of the list of laws because each of these laws, or features, necessarily produce the kinds of empowering life results we are looking to achieve.

Life coaching and working through each of the nine laws will invariably touch on all of them at the same time. As we move through this book, it will become evident that each phase of development, in one way or another, draws from some part of all of the nine laws of transformational life coaching.

Chapter 1 – Awareness

One of the first tenets of life coaching is cultivating awareness. An awareness of ourselves in the world is possibly the feature of the human condition that sets us apart from all other animals.

This basic understanding that we exist in a dynamic relationship with the world and with ourselves is a unique feature of human consciousness. It is so fundamental to our being that we take it for granted as if it is not changeable and something we can work on.

Transformative life coaching begins with the idea that this awareness, this basic feature of consciousness is something that we can impact, shape, and make our own. This stands out as the first law of transformative live coaching: the groundwork of Identitiy and how we begin to define our own identity. With this in mind, life coaches are able to take on specific issues in people's lives.

One person who underwent a system of coaching was experiencing anger issues. As he dealt with personality differences in the work place and especially with certain family members, he found that his anger would over-take all of his emotional well-being.

It was not as if he acted on the anger in an overt fashion. More to the point, his anger at others made it impossible for him to face a work day and cause him to shun specific members of his family. As life coaches, the first thing we need to do in a case such as this is demonstrate that his anger comes primarily from within.

We help people understand that though the actions and words of others are ultimately beyond our control, how we respond to these external triggers is entirely under our control.

Our awareness of ourselves in relation to others is the place to begin in a case such as this and life coaching teaches people focus their energies in these directions. The second law of coaching, then, would be defining the inside and the outside.

What are the external relations which define us and which external forces to we let control us?

In the case of this person with anger issues, he is almost certainly responding to old wounds within himself and to his own feelings of inadequacy in relation to others. Both of these things are built on faulty beliefs about himself.

The life coach here would implement a third law of transformative life coaching: that of limiting negative beleifs. By practicing empathy and mindfulness with the help of a transformational life coach, one is able to learn to deal with these sorts of internal struggles as they are manifested in relation to others.

The role of the life coach is to demonstrate that we can learn to manage external issues and pressures in ways that are more healthy and productive when we are led to be more aware of ourselves. This necessarily involves coaching people to become more open.

To reveal themselves in the safety of a life coaching environment so that they may become more aware of those points of vulnerability which are trigger points for them. We help people get in touch with their essential self—those features of the self which are most valued by the individual and most valuable to the world-- and this way they become more at ease with navigating the external world.

Chapter 2 – The Essential Self

The essential self which life coaches teach people to discover consists of those aspects of one's being which are most in line with one's personal self-ideal and also align with the kinds of life goals that person hopes to achieve.

That basic awareness we spoke of from the start consists of two fundamental drives: who do I need to be and who do I want to be? The tension between these two questions is the nexus of life coaching.

 Through the processes of awakening awareness, through the careful coaching through points of vulnerability, the life coach can resolve the antagonism between the outside and the inside.

From this basic awareness, life coaches begin to help the client by empowering their beliefs and instilling more positive beliefs in themselves. A Fourth law of life coaching is empowering beleifs. One life coach in particular addressed this issue with client as they dealt with friendship issues.

It was the outside demands versus the inside sense of self that were at odds and the point of vulnerability was precisely the place where this life coach saw the site for meaningful work and productive change for his client.

Again, here was a point at which the drive to be a specific type of person for a friend (who do I need to be) and the demand to be true to oneself (who do I want to be) were at odds and became the site for life coaching work.

This notion of the essential self is a complicated idea. It is obviously a psychological problem but for many it is also a spiritual question. Even from the perspective of psychology the essential self can be an elusive concept.

One study which takes this question form the vantage of mindfulness training, asserts that the essence of our being is a stable aspect of ourselves and that we encounter throughout our lives various road blocks which re-direct this essence away from itself.

In short, those forms of socialization that teach us to conform to rules, norms, and ideals which are in opposition to our essential self, will over-ride the self and leave a person a state of open ended internal conflict. Mindfulness asks clients questions pointed questions about what types of things stand in the way of who they wish to be.

While eschewing judgment, a life coach utilizing mindfulness will gather the answers to these questions and then gently guide the client through a process which dismantles these road blocks. This results in a two-fold process.

The client recognizes the fictive aspect of the blocks. With this a hole will emerge in their sense of self. This hole is then transformed into an open space for the client to begin the express the essential self that is within. These blocks are built on fears.

The most powerful tool for dispelling fears is learning to understand them. These methods and practices constitute a fifth law of life coaching: understanding fears.

From a spiritual perspective, the essential self exists as a universal constant. The human essential self exists as a spiritual feature of our being. It becomes constrained on various levels but that the essential self becomes expressed is ultimately inevitable.

For the life coach this can be invaluable to the extent that the essential self will emerge. As a life coach, we are to engage this through the other procedures and allow the inevitability of the spiritual self function as yet another power the client can tap into and master.

Through spiritual empowerment clients learn to transform fears into strength. The life coach utilizes this combination of understanding and spiritual guidance to set into place the sixth law of transformative life coaching: transforming fears.

Chapter 3 – Leaps of Faith

Three important features of life coaching are working through leaps of faith, trust, and dealing with the unknown.

As we encounter difficulties and struggles in our lives, we find that many of these struggles involve facing the unknown. We can shrink from this, and many of us do, or we can learn to embrace the unknown through trust in ourselves and by learning to take leaps of faith with the help of a qualified and competent life coach.

One example involves a client who found that their job was no longer relevant to the company they had worked for many years. This person's first response was to collapse in defeat.

The feeling of becoming irrelevant was overwhelming and they were ready to just give up on life. A crisis point in life such as this produces a host of negative emotions.

We turn on ourselves and see failure, an inability to keep pace with the world, even our own mortality can become bound up in a crisis of this type. However, this person utilized the skills of transformative life coaching in order to turn inward and examine the source of these negative feelings.

Rather that be a passive victim of circumstances and allow those circumstances to determine who to be, the person in this case took stock of what they were capable of, what they really wanted to do in life and re-direct all of the negative feelings and bleak outlook into an opportunity to transform their life. In this case, they went into transformative life coaching in particular.

All of this required a willingness to confront the unknown and take a leap of faith. Rather than shy away from the basic facts of their predicament, the person described above faced these facts and took serious stock of what these facts meant.

First, she came to the conclusion that she was anything but irrelevant. She was an accomplished, intelligent, and skilled adult with a tremendous amount to offer the world.

Second, she realized that the outcomes of any attempt todo things new and different are always unknown.

Therefore, the unknown was inevitable; why not confront the unknown with a prepared mind, take the leap of faith on a brand new direction in life and go forward prepared rather than afraid.

All of thie required the essential ideas and skills talked about at the beginning. She has to take stock of that basic antagonism between who the world defines here as opposed to how she defines herself.

She had to decide on specific goals with her essential self in mind. And finally, she had to proceed without allowing habitual fears intruding.

Since fear is such a basic human condition and because it is a primary impediment to realizing life goals, it makes sense to spend just a little time discussing this in particular. Fear is a natural response to danger. It is a necessary feature of being human.

This basic set of emotions is what leads us to protect ourselves and others. However, when fear becomes a habitual way of being in the world; when fears are based on what we imagine rather than what actually exists; and when fear prevents us from doing those things which lead us to our full potential, we must begin to find ways to manage and deal with fear.

In short, this client came to a powerful realization about themselves, her fears, and her relation to the world. This realization is a key aspect to the seventh law of life coaching. Realization means to see the reality of our world, as opposed to the world which consists of faulty beliefs. It also means to make real our goals and aspirations. Realization is the terms ofr this law.

Live coaching often begins with the process of determining and inventory of what we fear. One coach offers a step by step process for taking inventory of fears.

By taking time to meditate and become grounded, taking out a physical sheet of paper and a pen, and writing them out in the form of "I fear X…" until you come up with an exhaustive list, you can then begin to dismantle these fears.

By learning to visualize the fears, by seeing them before you, you can begin to understand how much of the fear is real and how much is imagined. By utilizing the methods of transformation life coaching, you can teach people how to deal with their fears and even how to be rid of them.

Utilizing something like the written inventory, or other method, we life coaches teach you how to approach the fears. The first thing to do is to understand them. The more we understand things, the less power they have over us.

Much of what consumes us in fear is speculation. We really do not know anything about the things we fear and will speculate or fill in the blanks with ideas that serve only to intensify the fear. This is using your imagination to create something you do not like and is a waste of our creative energies.

Transformational life coaching teaches people to research the things you are afraid of. Give names and definitions to things we know nothing about. In this way, the mind, the imagination can wrap itself around the fear and overcome it.

Another important way that fear takes us over is by our refusals to confront the fear. When we do not confront our fears we are, in essence, repressing those fears.

We all know the feeling of repressed laughter form our childhoods. Nothing accelerates that childish laughter faster than attempting to suppress it. Fear operates in an analogous way.

The more we deny these fears, the more control the fears have over us. The repressed or denied fear gets larger and more controlling.

A life coach will show people how to properly confront their fears. By placing ones dreams in dialogue with ones fears, a transformation life coach guides clients through the confrontation with their fears.

As a client is gently allowed to confront the fear through the process of educating themselves about that fear, along with a step by step analysis of the personal goals and dreams that his fear impedes, the life coach allows a client to overcome those fears and transform themselves from being afraid to living their dreams and goals.

Chapter 4 – Embracing Being

As we coach people through fears and external tensions, we must move people toward their most essential being as a way to coach them toward their potential and reach their goals. This involves the process of embracing Being.

Being in terms of what we mean in life coaching means the essential aspects of what we are. This is to distinguish our essential being from all the external definitions which are forced on us all our lives. Women, for example, grow up in a world which defines femininity and womanhood from a vast array of points of view—many of them rather damaging.

Woman are often taught to remain passive and silent, that their opinions are not valuable, and that they are too weak to deal with life struggles on their own. All of these beliefs are fallacies which can be crippling to women.

Life coaching aims to re-direct a woman's internal self-belief away from such destructive ideas toward more realistic and productive ideas The point is, women grow with and eventually assume these definitions of womanhood as themselves. Part of what transformative life coaching does is unravel these external definitions of selfhood and get to the core of what women want to be; in short, reveal the core of their essential being and then create methods to cultivate that essential being.

It is this feature of life coaching which involves limiting negative belief. We chose the example of women above but all of us are the result of negative beliefs. We mistake these beliefs as fundamental realities.

The goal of transformative life coaching is reveal these core beliefs as just that "beliefs" rather than realities. One specific method for working through these negative beliefs is the process of revelation and recognition. In this process, clients are coached to confront their negative beliefs about themselves, their lack of worth, lack of confidence, their sense of their own power, and then learn to recognize these beliefs.

Through a guided process of recognition, clients begin to isolate these ideas and see the source of them in external forces (social definitions, religions, family traditions, etc.).

They then go through the process of revelation in which the negative beliefs they hold a revealed to be illusory.

Once clients can go through these process a few times they begin to experience recognition and revelation on their own. Always the goal if life coaching is to guide a client to a point at which they assume control over their own lives and know how to apply the lessons and principles of life coaching on their own.

From the recognition and revelation of negative beliefs, transformative life coaches introduce the process of empowering belief. To a certain degree this stage of life coaching boils down to a simple dichotomy: what you believe you can do and what you believe you should do.

Relying on the idea that "I should" do one thing or another is destructive to our essential being. The drive of "Should" is never from within; it is always a function and directive of the will of others. It is true that as adults there are an endless series of responsibilities and contingencies that we have to attend to and these are, in some measure, things we "should" do.

But basic adult responsibility to others is a feature of maturity and it needs to be distinguished from mandates that tell us what we should do which are contrary to our sense of self and the beliefs we hold dear. We should take care of those we love because we are responsible for their well-being. We made that promise to them.

There is nothing that says we should conform to the demands of others that we dress a specific way, that we keep our mouths shut in the face of things we find objectionable, that we conform to standards of femininity and masculinity that is not an expression of our essential being. This is the core distinction transformative life coaches need to make.

This stage in life coaching can be said to be the "transformative "phase." It consists largely of points of identification. The client identifies negative beliefs and fears, the sources of those beleifs, and ultimately identifies the essential self they already are at the their core.

The multi-fold process of indentifying stands as an eighth law of life coaching. A life coach will at this stage ask a client to name two or more positive and affirming beliefs and imagine limitless possibilities that can come from internalizing and living these beliefs.

Clients are asked to meditate on these beliefs and visualize them for a period of time. This brings to the fore new perspectives on possibilities and on the self. The client will begin to see the world around them and themselves in light of these new and affirming beliefs.

This is a gradual process. Old habitual belief systems do not simply disappear and in fact, however destructive many of these beliefs are, they can be deceptively comfortable simply because a client has lived them all their lives.

But through the visualizing process, through periods of meditation guided by an experienced life coach, the new beliefs begin to take hold and the essential being the client needs to recognize and reveal emerges. This is the transformative feature of life coaching.

As you can see, the process is both holistic and builds on a scaffold of interconnected aspects of essential being. Fears are the result of ingrained ideas and habitual modes of feeling.

They are also a feature of external definitions of one's inner self or inner being.

By revealing the illusory nature of fears, and by revealing the external source of self-definition, transformative life coaches can guide a person toward a revelatory experience in which their inner sense and self-determined sense of being is revealed and allowed to flourish.

Chapter 5 – The Hierarchy of Commitment

All of this consists of a general hierarchy of commitment. What coaches require from clients is willingness—willingness to listen, to take chances, and to allow the coach to form transpersonal connections via the processes of recognition and revelation.

The most basic level of commitment is willingness. From here coaches are able to establish binds with their clients. A general unfolding through inquiry, a second level of the hierarchy, involves a focused period of asking questions. Through this period of inquiry the transformational life coach can dig below a client's defenses and habitual forms of belief.

This process is delicate and requires tremendous empathy. This also demands the coaches withhold their own personal values and judgments. It is crucial that coaches bear in mind that the goal of this time of inquiry is to uncover the deeper structures of belief which give rise to the client's fears.

The standards of judgment that have conditioned client to view themselves in specific way and to view the world in specific ways. Remember, much of this internal belief system will be the basis for all that is to be transformed. If a coach betrays any of their own judgments, the client will guard themselves and this is entirely counterproductive.

Finally, there is the very practical element of problem solving. This may or may not lead to actual solutions to the client's problems, but this stage will lead the client to find ways of handling problems.

One of the most common motivating factors which leads a person to consult a life coach is a mass of problems, some real, some perceived, which the client has come see as insurmountable. Often a person will approach a life coach as a consultant for solving their problems. The role of the coach at this stage is to take all of the tools and lessons from the entire process and apply them to practical real-life issues.

A client may not be able to finally erase their, for example, but with the tools, confidence and self-assurance that comes with thorough life coaching, the client can find and implement strategies for dealing with debt. Transformational life coaching ultimately about empowerment more than fixing problems.

Chapter 6 – Methods and Tools

How does the life coach achieve these steps? How do we gain access to another person and establish the trust necessary to guide them through what may well be some painful moments?

One key method is story telling. All of us recount moments form our lives as narratives.

This can be a simple as relating a silly moment to a friend at work. We share powerful moments form our lives in the form of stories with those who become close to us. This feature of human interaction is the process of story-telling and this can be a powerful tool for coaching people through life crises and difficulties.

Much of how we come view ourselves comes in the form of stories. What most of us tend to overlook is the fact that we do not just become the protagonists of our stories; we are also the primary interpreter of this story.

The role of the life coach in utilizing the story for clients is to allow the client to tell their story. The coach listens intently, again free of judgment. We gather the information this story presents us with and we become particularly attentive to the value the client places on this story.

A memory from childhood can be recounted with all of the innocence of childhood, but the story may well contain aspects of the current status of the client.

One of the key insights of life coaching is that we are not our stories. We are a collection of stories, this is true, but we are not essentially these stories. Life coaching involves re-interpreting the stories that make up a clients history with the present clearly in focus.

Our past, the stories which make up our past, are not happening now. We are in the present and life coaches can intervene in the interpretation of the client's life story so as to guide the narrative toward the present situations and the present goals.

Those moments which involved the transformation of negative emotions into positive actions will come into play at this stage. Remember, all points of engagement are moments for transformation.

A memory of parental disapproval is an invitation to validate the childhood confusion and re-direct the negative feelings associated with that memory, turning them into empowering tools for future work. The life coach relieves the client of responsibility, for example, from childhood or early adult crisis moments.

Another useful method is the use of a three-pronged approach called Spheres of influence. In this exercise the life coach helps a client break down the various dimensions of their life into three categories:

Things we can control.

Things we can influence.

Things we cannot influence, either right now or at all times.

From this the coach can guide a person into prioritizing the various features of their life into manageable forms. Those things we can control can be immediately confronted.

The fears and negative emotions which may prevent this confrontation will necessarily become the next space of guidance. Things we can influence will give rise to strategy brain-storming sessions with the life coach. Here the concept of openness will become essential.

Those things we cannot influence will of necessity compel the coach and the client to work out strategies of coping. However, this last category can be the most liberating for a client because with the inability to influence something, the client is also absolved of responsibility for those things.

One more important tool for many life coaches is to encourage clients to use a personal journal. The advantages of a personal journal for life coaching cannot be over-emphasized. Clients may believe they have their thoughts and ideas collected and organized but the reality is that almost none of us really are that organized.

None of us can even retain all the thoughts and feelings that influence in any given day. By writing in a personal journal, free of other eyes, free of the fear of judgment that can come from speaking things out loud, clients can begin to see their own thoughts and feelings before their own eyes. As a life coach it is important that you never demand to see the journal.

Their journal is for their own recognitions and revelations. They should be expected to discuss what is in the journal but their words are their own. In this way, a client can express thoughts, ideas, feelings, memories, etc. as freely as possible.

Through journaling, a client may come to see that something they believed was small and trivial is in fact of crucial importance to their current outlook on life. A personal journal can give the client and the life coach the basic building blocks for all of the other steps in life coaching.

The unifying feature of all of these methods is to pull together all the other aspects of transformative life coaching. These methods are tools to implement the first eight laws and to make use of all the other lessons and features. As We have already seen, life coaching is a holistic process. We do not practive life coaching like a school teacher.

Each law, and each practive is imtimately linked to the others. Thus the ninth law of transformative life coaching is overall empowerment.The client will feel a sense of self empowerment from the holistic processes and methods of the entire process.

Conclusion

The basic tenets of life coaching are here. We see how the nine laws of life coaching unfold in a natural order in which each law gives rise to the next. There is a vast array of methodologies and styles available. What we have covered here is a general overview which should point anyone in the right direction toward becoming a transformational life coach.

There are entire forms of life coaching specifically tailored to the needs of women, for example. In our contemporary world, the specific issues women confront and are confronted with demand that specific models conform to these needs.

Still other methods of life coaching are geared toward the work place. May employers have found that the conflicts and road blocks specific to the work place can in fact be dealt with in an effective way by utilizing the methods of a transformational life coach.

What is most important for a reader to take form this book is accessibility of this growing field. It requires empathy and great deal of patience. Life coaches must be able to let go of their own personal need to be liked. Some of what coaches must do in the course of working with a client involved helping the client deal with harsh truths and harsh realities.

A life coach must be equipped to present these things knowing that the client may initially react to them in a negative way. Since you are committed to coaching your client to realizing their highest potential, you must be committed to holding the client to this work.

Transformational life coaching demands a certain amount of stamina. With empathy, the life coach must also remain detached to the extent that the client is free to determine his or her own goals.

 We must not prescribe goals for them. This means that life coaches need to be able to hold back their own desires and ideals with respect to a client's particular needs and desires. Finally, the life coach must be able to suspend his or her ego. The work we do is empowering our clients. We are not in the business of showing them how intelligent we are or how insightful we can be.

If we adhere to these nine laws of life coaching, the client will feel themselves taking over their own life and their own destiny.